FOOD LOVERS

SMOOTHIES & JUICES

RECIPES SELECTED BY JONNIE LÉGER

Trans
Atlantic
Press

For best results when cooking the recipes in this book, buy fresh ingredients and follow the instructions carefully. Note that as a general rule vulnerable groups such as the very young, elderly people, pregnant women, convalescents and anyone suffering from an illness should avoid dishes that contain raw or lightly cooked eggs.

For all recipes, quantities are given in standard U.S. cups and imperial measures, followed by the metric equivalent. Follow one set or the other, but not a mixture of both because conversions may not be exact. Standard spoon and cup measurements are level and are based on the following:

1 tsp. = 5 ml, 1 tbsp. = 15 ml, 1 cup = 250 ml / 8 fl oz.

Note that Australian standard tablespoons are 20 ml, so Australian readers should use 3 tsp. in place of 1 tbsp. when measuring small quantities.

CONTENTS

RASPBERRY AND ACAI BERRY SMOOTHIE

Ingredients

Serves 2

1¼ cups / 300 ml acai berry juice

12 oz / 350 g frozen raspberries

1 cup / 250 g natural yogurt

2 tbsp runny honey

To garnish:

Some raspberries

1 tsp demerara sugar

Method

Prep and cook time: 10 min

1 Put the acai berry juice into a blender. Add the frozen raspberries, yogurt and honey.

2 Whiz together until blended and really smooth. Pour into 2 glasses.

3 Dip the ends of 6 raspberries into the smoothie, then dip these raspberry tips into the demerara sugar. Thread the raspberries onto wooden skewers or cocktail sticks to serve.

RASPBERRY AND PEACH DRINK

Ingredients
Serves 2

1 peach, coarsely chopped

½ cup / 100 g raspberries

2 tbsp honey

1 tbsp flaked (slivered) almonds

2 tsp lemon juice

¼ cup / 50 ml grape juice

6 ice cubes

Well chilled sparkling mineral water,
as needed

Method
Prep and cook time: 5 min

1 Place the peach, raspberries, honey, almonds, lemon juice, grape juice and ice cubes in a blender and pulse to a smooth purée.

2 Divide between 2 glasses; add mineral water to fill.

VANILLA SMOOTHIE

Ingredients
Serves 2

½ cup / 75 g cubed honeydew melon

1 firm banana, cut into chunks

1 cup / 250 g plain yogurt

1 vanilla bean, slit lengthwise and seeds scraped out

8 ice cubes

1/3 – ½ cup / 100 ml whipping cream

1 tbsp lime juice, or to taste

2 tsp brown sugar

Method
Prep and cook time: 15 min

1 Place the melon, banana, yogurt and vanilla seeds into a blender and pulse until smooth.

2 Continue blending, gradually adding the cream and ice cubes, until very creamy. Add lime juice to taste.

3 Divide the smoothie between 2 glasses and sprinkle with brown sugar.

4 Using a cook's blowtorch, caramelize the sugar on the surface of the smoothies and serve at once.

CAPPUCCINO SMOOTHIE

Ingredients

Serves 2

1¼ cups / 300 ml strong
espresso coffee

2 handfuls crushed ice

1¼ cups / 300 ml milk

2 tbsp maple syrup

2 tsp dark chocolate, finely grated

Method

Prep and cook time: 5 min plus 30 min cooling time

1 Pour the espresso coffee into a jug and cool.

2 Put a couple of handfuls of crushed ice into a blender and add the coffee, milk and maple syrup.

3 Whiz everything together until smooth.

4 Pour into 2 glasses and sprinkle over the finely grated chocolate to serve.

GINGER DRINK

Ingredients

Serves 2

4 inch / 10 cm piece fresh ginger root, coarsely grated (reserve juice)

2 tbsp brown sugar

1 large lemon

2 cups / 475 ml sparkling mineral water

Fresh mint sprigs, to garnish

Method

Prep and cook time: 10 min plus 10 min standing time

1 Put the ginger and its juice into a pitcher (jug) and sprinkle in the sugar.

2 Zest and juice the lemon, then add the zest to the pitcher and mash with a pestle or with the tip of a rolling pin. Pour the lemon juice into the pitcher.

3 Pour in the sparkling water. Allow to stand for 10 minutes; taste and add a little more sugar, if necessary.

4 Strain the ginger drink through a sieve and divide between 2 glasses with lots of ice and some sprigs of mint.

CARROT AND PINEAPPLE JUICE

Ingredients

Serves 2

1 pineapple, trimmed and peeled

2 carrots, trimmed

1 zucchini (courgette), trimmed

Method

Prep and cook time: 10 min

1 Quarter the pineapple and cut away the central woody core. Cut into long thin wedges.

2 Put a glass under the juicer spout and press half the pineapple, carrots and zucchinni (courgette) through the juicer.

3 Remove the filled glass and place another glass under the juicer spout. Press the remaining pineapple, carrots and zucchini through the machine and serve.

COCONUT AND BERRY SMOOTHIE

Ingredients
Serves 2

$1/3$ cup / 50 g blueberries

$1/3$ cup / 50 g redcurrants

2 tbsp brown sugar

3 tbsp desiccated coconut, toasted in a dry pan and cooled

$1/3 – 1/2$ cup / 100 ml coconut milk

Generous $3/4$ cup / 200 ml milk

Method
Prep and cook time: 10 min plus 30 mins chilling

1 Lay the blueberries and redcurrants in a shallow dish and place in the freezer for about 30 minutes.

2 Purée the berries, sugar, 2 tbsp of the desiccated coconut, coconut milk and milk in a blender.

3 Pour into two glasses and serve sprinkled with the remaining desiccated coconut.

MANGO AND PINEAPPLE SMOOTHIE

Ingredients

Serves 2

2 large, ripe mangos, peeled

Juice of 1 lime, zest peeled off in thin strips and reserved

A few ice cubes

$1/3 - 1/2$ cup / 100 ml pineapple juice

1–2 tbsp honey

Well-chilled still mineral water, if required

Garnish:

Fresh mint leaves

Reserved lime zest

Method

Prep and cook time: 10 min plus 30 min chilling time

1 Cut the flesh away from either side of the mango stone and chop the flesh.

2 Lay the chopped mango in a shallow dish and place in the freezer for about 30 minutes.

3 Whiz the mango, lime juice, ice cubes, pineapple juice and honey in a blender. Well-chilled water can be added if necessary.

4 Divide the smoothie between 2 glasses and garnish with the strips of lime zest and mint leaves.

CHILI MANGO COCKTAIL

Ingredients

Serves 2

1 red chili, sliced and deseeded

2 tbs lime juice

4 tsp agave syrup

$1/3 - 1/2$ cup / 100 ml elderflower cordial (made up from 2–3 tbsp of undiluted cordial plus cold water)

2 cups / 450 ml mango juice

4 handfuls ice cubes

4 tbsp grenadine

To garnish:

2 red chilies

2 sticks mango flesh, cut from a fresh fruit

Method

Prep and cook time: 15 min

1 Put the chili slices into a cocktail shaker and mash (muddle) with a long spoon.

2 Add the lime juice, agave syrup, elderflower cordial, mango juice and 2 handfuls of ice.

3 Pour the grenadine into the bottom of 2 tall glasses and add the rest of the ice.

4 Shake the cocktail shaker well and strain the juice into the glasses.

5 Garnish each glass with a chili and a stick of mango.

PEACH AND PASSION FRUIT SMOOTHIE

Ingredients
Serves 2

1 lb / 450 g can peaches in natural juice

1 banana, sliced

$^2/_3$ cup / 150 ml passion fruit juice

$^2/_3$ cup / 150 ml low fat milk

1 passion fruit, halved, to garnish

Method
Prep and cook time: 5 min

1 In a blender or food processor, combine the canned peaches and their juice, banana, passion fruit juice and milk. Pulse until completely smooth and pour into 2 glasses.

2 Scoop out the passion fruit seeds and spoon them on top of each smoothie to garnish.

LEMON GRASS LEMONADE

Ingredients

Serves 2

1 stem lemon grass

Zest and juice of 2 large lemons

¼ cup / 50 g superfine (caster) sugar

2½ cups / 600 ml boiling water

10 ice cubes

Garnish:

2 stems lemon grass

2 mint sprigs

Method

Prep and cook time: 15 min plus 8 hours chilling

1 Trim off the base and top of the lemon grass stem; finely slice the remainder. Put the sliced lemon grass into a heatproof bottle or container and add the lemon juice, zest and sugar.

2 Pour over the boiling water. Cover and let steep overnight.

3 Stir and taste for sweetness, adding more sugar if needed. Strain the lemonade into 2 glasses.

4 Add ice cubes to fill and garnish with a lemon grass stem and mint sprig in each glass.

ICED FRUIT COCKTAIL

Ingredients

Serves 2

1 cup / 200 g mixed fruit (try grapefruit, apple, black grapes) cut into bite-size pieces

1 cup / 250 ml apple juice

2 tbsp lime juice

6 ice cubes

About 1 cup / 200 ml well-chilled sparkling mineral water

Method

Prep and cook time: 10 min

1 Thread the prepared fruit onto wooden skewers.

2 Pour the apple juice and lime juice into a blender. Add the ice cubes and pulse briefly.

3 Divide the juice between two glasses and add the fruit skewers. Add mineral water to fill.

STRAWBERRY AND ALMOND SMOOTHIE

Ingredients

Serves 2

1 cup / 200 g ripe strawberries, hulled (reserve a few, sliced, for garnish)

2 tbsp ground almonds

2 tbsp elderflower liqueur

1¼ cups / 300 g cold plain yogurt

Garnish:

Flaked almonds

Strawberry slices

Method

Prep and cook time: 15 min plus 30 min chilling time

1 Place the strawberries in a shallow dish and put in the freezer for 30 minutes until partially frozen.

2 Place the strawberries, ground almonds, liqueur and the yogurt in a blender and pulse until creamy.

3 Divide between 2 glasses and garnish with flaked almonds and strawberry slices.

CARROT AND MANGO JUICE

Ingredients
Serves 2

2 large carrots, peeled

1¼ cups / 300 ml cold water

1 mango, peeled and chopped

²/₃ cup / 150 ml orange juice

Garnish:

1 celery stick, quartered

4 walnut halves

Method
Prep and cook time: 10 min plus 20 min standing time

1 Grate the carrots and put into a bowl with the cold water. Cover and leave for 20 minutes.

2 Put the mango into a blender with the orange juice. Pulse until smooth.

3 Hold a sieve over the blender and strain the carrot juice into it, discarding the shredded carrots. Pulse again to combine.

4 Pour into 2 glasses and garnish each with celery stalks and a couple of walnut halves.

PEAR YOGURT SHAKE WITH CINNAMON

Ingredients
Serves 2

1 medium-sized ripe pear, peeled, quartered, cored and chopped

Scant cup / 200 ml plain yogurt

$2/3$ cup / 150 ml whipping cream

1 tbsp acacia honey

½ tsp ground cinnamon

1 pinch nutmeg

Cinnamon sugar, to garnish

Method
Prep and cook time: 10 min

1 Put the pear, yogurt, cream, honey, cinnamon and nutmeg in a blender and pulse until smooth. For best results, the pear should be soft but not mushy. Yogurt and cream should be well chilled.

2 Pour into 2 glasses and sprinkle with cinnamon sugar to serve.

TOMATO GAZPACHO SMOOTHIE

Ingredients

Serves 2

14-oz / 400 g can diced tomatoes in juice

½ red bell pepper, seeded

½ cucumber, chopped

1 tbsp balsamic vinegar

1 tbsp cilantro (coriander leaves)

1 scallion (spring onion), chopped

1 garlic clove, peeled

Dash chili sauce

Crushed ice, as needed

Garnish:

2 watercress sprigs

Method

Prep and cook time: 20 min

1 In a blender, combine the tomatoes, bell pepper, cucumber, balsamic vinegar, cilantro (coriander leaves), scallion (spring onion), garlic and chili sauce.

2 Add a couple of handfuls of crushed ice and pulse until smooth.

3 Pour into 2 glasses and garnish each one with a watercress sprig.

CHERRY AND CRANBERRY SMOOTHIE

Ingredients
Serves 2

1 cup / 250 g frozen pitted dark sweet cherries

1¼ cups / 300 ml sweetened cranberry juice

1¼ cups / 300 g low-fat cherry yogurt

Method
Prep and cook time: 5 min

1 Put the frozen cherries, cranberry juice and yogurt into a blender and pulse into smooth.

2 Pour into 2 glasses to serve.

BERRY AND POMEGRANATE LASSI

Ingredients
Serves 2

½ cup / 100 g frozen raspberries

½ cup / 100 g frozen blackcurrants

¼ cup / 50 g strawberries, hulled

1¼ cups / 300 g low-fat plain yogurt

1¼ cups / 300 ml pomegranate juice

Garnish:

2 tbsp chopped fresh mint leaves

Method
Prep and cook time: 10 min

1 Put the frozen raspberries, blackcurrants and strawberries, yogurt and pomegranate juice into a blender. Pulse until smooth.

2 Pour into 2 glasses and sprinkle over the chopped mint to garnish.

BANOFFEE TOFFEE MILKSHAKE

Ingredients

Serves 2

2 bananas, sliced

2 cups / 500 ml milk

4 tbsp dulce de leche caramel*

2 scoops caramel ice cream

Garnish:

2 pecans, chopped

Method

Prep and cook time: 5 min

1 Put the bananas into a blender and add the milk, caramel and ice cream. Pulse until smooth.

2 Pour into 2 glasses and sprinkle over the pecans to garnish.

*Dulce de leche, an intensely sweet milk caramel made by boiling down sweetened milk, can be found in gourmet stores.

BELL PEPPER AND PAPAYA JUICE

Ingredients

Serves 2

4 red bell peppers, halved and seeded

2 papayas, peeled, seeded and coarsely chopped

Juice of 1 lime

Garnish:

Celery stalks

Method

Prep and cook time: 15 min

1 Push the bell peppers and papayas down the feeder tube of a juicer into 2 glasses.

2 Add the juice of half a lime to each glass; stir and serve garnished with a celery stalk.

HEALTHY EGG AND WHEAT GERM SMOOTHIE

Ingredients

Serves 2

2 very fresh eggs, separated

2 tbsp acacia honey

1²/₃ cups / 400 ml whole milk

2 tbsp wheat germ

Freshly grated nutmeg

Ground cinnamon

Method

Prep and cook time: 20 min

1 With an electric mixer, beat the egg yolks and honey in a bowl until pale and frothy; set aside.

2 In a small saucepan, heat the milk, stirring, over medium-high heat until bubbles form at the edge of the pan (do not allow the milk to boil). Set aside to cool slightly.

3 In another bowl with a whisk or an electric mixer, beat the egg whites until stiff.

4 Add the warm milk and wheat germ to the egg yolk mixture and combine with an immersion (hand-held) blender until smooth and homogeneous.

5 Add nutmeg and cinnamon to taste, then fold in the stiff egg whites. Divide between 2 glasses and serve immediately.

WARM APPLE PUNCH

Ingredients

Serves 2

2 cups / 500 ml apple juice

1 cinnamon stick

4 juniper berries

Zest and juice of 1 orange

Garnish:

Red apple peel

2 cinnamon sticks

Method

Prep and cook time: 30 min

1 Put the apple juice, cinnamon stick and juniper berries into a large saucepan.

2 Add the orange juice and zest to the saucepan; bring to a boil, reduce the heat and simmer for 20 minutes to infuse the spices.

3 Strain the punch and ladle into 2 heatproof glasses. Garnish each with a cinnamon stick and a swirl of apple peel.

Published by Transatlantic Press

First published in 2011

Transatlantic Press
38 Copthorne Road, Croxley Green, Hertfordshire WD3 4AQ

© Transatlantic Press

Images and Recipes by StockFood © The Food Image Agency

Recipes selected by Jonnie Léger, StockFood

A catalogue record for this book is available from the British Library.

ISBN 978-1-908533-64-7

Printed in China